Rejoice in Hope

Thriving in a Spiritual Recession

Edward Kleinguetl

Rejoice in Hope
Thriving in a Spiritual Recession
All Rights Reserved.
Copyright © 2023 Edward Kleinguetl
v2.0

The opinions expressed in this manuscript are solely the opinions of the author and do not represent the opinions or thoughts of the publisher. The author has represented and warranted full ownership and/or legal right to publish all the materials in this book.

This book may not be reproduced, transmitted, or stored in whole or in part by any means, including graphic, electronic, or mechanical without the express written consent of the publisher except in the case of brief quotations embodied in critical articles and reviews.

Outskirts Press, Inc.
http://www.outskirtspress.com

ISBN: 978-1-9772-6035-2

Cover Photo © 2023. Dreamstime. All rights reserved – used with permission.

Outskirts Press and the "OP" logo are trademarks belonging to Outskirts Press, Inc.

PRINTED IN THE UNITED STATES OF AMERICA

*I have a single burning desire: to change the world
by changing a single person—myself.*

—St. Sophrony of Essex

*Problems! Problems! We will solve them together
… But if we turn our eyes a little toward heaven,
we will see that there is only one problem:
the salvation of our soul.*

—Elder Eusebius Giannakakis

*Compel yourself; rise to your stature; prove that you
are a disciple of Christ and not of the devil.*

—Elder Ephraim of Arizona

*By self-denial, the man who follows Christ is resurrected
spiritually; he comes out of the grave of his own selfishness and
becomes filled with the merciful and humble love of Christ.*

—Patriarch Daniel of Romania

Table of Contents

Introduction:
    Spiritual Recession 1

Conferences:
    Rejoice in Hope 3
    Endure in Affliction 19
    Persevere in Prayer 37

Conclusion:
    Recession-Proofing Our Lives 47

Supplemental Information:
    Calling on the Sweet Name of Jesus 49

Bibliography 51

INTRODUCTION

Spiritual Recession

"Rejoice in hope, endure in affliction, persevere in prayer."
(Rom. 12:12)

"My child, encourage your soul and be hopeful." [1]
(Elder Ephraim of Arizona)

We all know the signs of an economic recession: contraction instead of growth, rising prices, rising interest rates, declining individual purchasing power, and a general feeling of dread and uncertainty. It is hitting a wall. However, there is an even greater downturn afflicting our culture. We are in a spiritual recession of epic proportions: faith is cooling, people are lost, and many have separated themselves from God, the true Source of Life. Souls are at risk, and many are dying.

We see the signs, too, of this spiritual recession, and some of us are weighed down by them. We may have feelings of angst and despair. That is because the secular world, now more than ever, attempts to drown out the Good News of the Gospel: Jesus Christ lived, died, and rose so that we could be free from sin and death. He came to bring us life, the abundant life.[2] Giving into the world will leave us with difficulties and empty promises. Yet, as Jesus told us, "Take courage, I have conquered the world."[3] As true Christians, we live in the world, but we are not *of* the world, nor is this our ultimate home. What we are experiencing now will pass away. Elder Ephraim of Arizona said:

---

1 *Counsels from the Holy Mountain: Selected from the Letters and Homilies of Geronda Ephraim of Arizona*, 2nd ed., trans. from Greek (Florence, AZ: St. Anthony's Greek Orthodox Monastery, 2022), 273. "Geronda" is a title meaning "elder" in Greek.
2 John 10:10. All biblical quotes contained herein are from the NABRE, 2011, unless otherwise specified.
3 John 16:33.

Rejoice in Hope

> Do you not forget your goal, my child. Look into heaven and see the beauty that awaits us. What are the present, earthly things? Aren't they but dust and ashes and a dream? Don't we see that everything here is subject to decay? Whereas things above are everlasting, the Kingdom of God is endless, and blessed is he who will dwell in it, for he will behold the glory of his divine face![4]

For our retreat, we will reflect on the advice given by St. Paul in his Letter to the Romans: "Rejoice in hope, endure in affliction, persevere in prayer."[5] These words were addressed to Christians who were struggling, persecuted, and shunned. They are equally appropriate amid today's modern-day challenges. As we enter into this time of introspection, let us keep in mind that Jesus guarantees our hope. He is our surety. Do we feel hopefully? Or are we overcome with despair? Let us pinpoint where we are in our individual journeys and consider how we can thrive in this time of spiritual recession.

---

[4] *Counsels from the Holy Mountain*, 5.
[5] Rom. 12:12.

RETREAT CONFERENCE

Rejoice in Hope

"Always be ready to give an explanation to anyone who asks you for a reason for your hope."
(1 Pet. 3:15)

"Consider, beloved, how the Lord keeps reminding us of the resurrection that is to come, of which he has made the Lord Jesus Christ the firstfruits by raising him from the dead." [6]
(St. Clement of Rome)

Opening Retreat Prayer

Heavenly King, Comforter, Spirit of Truth, everywhere present and filling all things, Treasury of Blessings, and Giver of Life, come and dwell within us, cleanse of all stain, and save our souls, O Gracious One.

Lord, Jesus Christ, open our hearts and minds to hear your voice. Speak tenderly to those who call upon your name. Speak, Lord, your servants are listening.

Opening Reading: The Light of the Human Race

A reading from the Holy Gospel according to St. John:

In the beginning was the Word, and the Word was with God, and the Word was God. He was in the beginning with God. All things came to be through him, and without him nothing came to be.

---

[6] St. Clement of Rome, "Letter to the Corinthians," in *The Liturgy of the Hours*, vol. 4 (New York, NY: Catholic Book Publishing Corp, 1975), 448.

> What came to be through him was life, and this life was the light of the human race; the light shines in the darkness, and the darkness has not overcome it.

The Gospel of the Lord.

Heaven is Our True Home

Who wants to go to heaven? I am sure that many would say, "Yes, sign me up." However, do we make heaven the number one priority in our lives? Is it the North Star that guides us, day-in and day-out? Heaven cannot simply be one of our priorities, it must be *the* priority. Our concern must always be the salvation of our souls.

Statistics confirming we are in a spiritual recession are unmistakable. For every million children who are baptized, only 110,000 remain active in their faith by young adulthood. Over two-thirds of Catholics (69 percent) do not believe in the Real Presence of Christ in the Eucharist.[7] "Churches are emptying, but clinics prescribing anti-depressants are full."[8] Souls are dying! Many see God and Christianity as a means of enslavement, taking away our freedom, and are overtly hostile to the institutional Church and its teachings. These signs confirm this recession is deep and widespread.

We have heard the term RINO—Republicans in Name Only. Today, we have ChINOs, Christians in Name Only, those who want to remold God into their image, whom they think he *should* be. Others try to "modernize" the teachings of Christ, trying to widen the narrow gate in order to accommodate immoral or perverse behaviors. We even witness public officials claiming a strong Catholic faith and

---

[7] Gregory A. Smith, "Just One-Third of U.S. Catholics Agree with Their Church that Eucharist is Body, Blood of Christ," Pew Research Center, online, August 5, 2019. Survey was conducted February 4-19, 2022, among adult Catholics.

[8] Cf. St. Paisios the Athonite, "Spiritual Struggle," *Spiritual Counsels*, vol. 3, trans. Fr. Peter Chamberas, ed. Anna Famellos and Andronikos Masters (Souroti, Thessaloniki, Greece: Holy Hesychasterion Evangelist John the Theologian, 2014), 301. "Without good Spiritual Fathers, the churches empty, while the psychiatric wards, prisons, and hospitals become busier than ever. People need to realize that their life is troubled because they have distanced themselves from God; they need to realize they must repent and humbly confess their sins."

embracing positions that are fundamentally opposed to the teachings of the Church. Do we recognize the signs of times, or will Jesus rightly criticize us: "You hypocrites! You know how to interpret the appearance of the earth and the sky; why do you not know how to interpret the present time?"[9]

Let us each pause, carefully look around, and consider where we are. Have we grown rich in what matters to God?[10] Or have we stored up treasures on earth that, as Jesus warned, "Moth and decay destroy, and thieves break in and steal?"[11] What is the balance in our account today? Jesus tells us, "For where your treasure is, there also will your heart be."[12] So, where do we stand? Is our portfolio in a positive or negative position? Are we going spiritually bankrupt?

Now imagine that our time in this life has suddenly come to an end and we are called to make an account before the fearsome judgment seat of Christ. How will our souls be assessed by the just judge? This brings us back to our question: "Do we want to go to heaven?" Have we given our single-most important priority sufficient focus? Or will we be found lacking?

God wants to share his abundant life with us. He sent his Son to show us the way to that life. Yet, our effort is required. We must struggle; we must demonstrate to God that we want this life more than anything else. It is freely offered, but not freely given. We have a choice to make, which Jesus described well: "The kingdom of heaven is like a merchant searching for fine pearls. When he finds a pearl of great price, he goes and sells all that he has and buys it."[13] This is how we should see the prioritization of heaven. It is more valuable than anything else. St. Paisios the Athonite said, "The spiritual person does not aspire to anything other than the salvation of his soul."[14] Yet, let us

---

9   Luke 12:56.
10 Cf. Luke 12:21.
11 Matt. 6:19.
12 Matt. 6:21.
13 Matt. 13:45-6.
14 St. Paisios the Athonite, "On Prayer," *Spiritual Counsels*, vol. 6, trans. Fr. Peter Chamberas, ed. Anna Famellos and Eleftheria Kaimakliotis (Vasilika, Thessaloniki, Greece: Holy Hesychasterion Evangelist John the Theologian, 2022), 267.

be honest. How often are we willing to make the necessary choices, making heaven our priority, even when it is inconvenient? Or does a more immediate concern often take precedence? In rank order, what consumes our daily efforts?

God's Unconditional Love is Our Hope

There is one constant in life: God's unconditional love for humanity, his most prized creation, and this love secures our hope. Even though humanity rejected God and sinned, God sent his Only Son into the world to draw us back to him. Consider the significance of this event, Jesus emptying himself and taking on our humanity. The Incarnation is a historical event; it is both irrevocable and irreversible because God himself has acted in the world.[15] Christ accomplished his redeeming work during his time on Earth, and it continues to play out in historical time. Archbishop Joseph Raya adds:

> Without this Incarnation, in which the Son of God, God himself, became the Son of man and specifically Son of a human mother, Mary, Christianity has neither meaning nor relevance.[16]

Through the Incarnation, the Son of God became the Son of Man, and we have the possibility of becoming children of God.[17] We can be united to God through all eternity—the abundant life God wants to share with us. This is the Good News of the Gospel and the source of all hope.

Yet we might still wonder whether God truly really loves us. We endure hardships and generally make a mess of things. In response, let us consider the Crucifixion. Our arrogance crucified Jesus. Rather than recognizing Jesus as God's offer of salvation,

---

[15] Karl Rahner, *Foundations of Christian Faith: An Introduction to the Idea of Christianity*, trans. William V. Dych (New York, NY: Crossroad Publishing Company, 1990) 195.
[16] Archbishop Joseph M. Raya, *The Face of God: Essays on Byzantine Spirituality* (Woodland Park, NJ: God With Us Publications, 2012), 23.
[17] See John 1:12.

the Jewish authorities preferred the status quo, their traditions, following rigorous rules, and labeling most of the population as sinners. They liked the delusion that God rewarded virtuous living with prosperity[18] and prestige[19]—which is why they detested the teachings of Jesus that said God loved the poor and oppressed. Jesus stood in stark contrast to everything the religious leaders of his time held dear, and they simply could not accept it. So, they condemned Jesus to die, failing to recognize the truth of God's love in our midst.

Reflect on the cruelty experienced by Jesus: the scourging; beatings; crowning with thorns; the brutality and physical manhandling by the soldiers; insults; being spat upon; crushed by the weight of cross; stripped; publicly humiliated; and forced to die by being nailed to a cross—one of the most inhumane means of torture. We rejected God's love … and Jesus asked that we be forgiven, justifying our actions, saying that we did not know what we were doing.[20] The Crucifixion of Christ is our false judgment, wherein we rejected the truth. Yet, with this in mind, consider how God reacts to our false judgment and arrogance.

God responds with his overflowing love and forgiveness as manifested in the Resurrection. This is the truth of the depth of God's love for his creation and establishes the bedrock for our salvation. God still responded with love, even when we were at our worst. This is the source of our hope. Christ's Resurrection is victory over death and meaninglessness, affirmed at Pentecost with the outpouring of the Holy Spirit upon the Church, forming believers into the body of Christ. The Holy Spirit makes Christ's "yes" to the Father our "yes."[21]

God's love for us is the one constant that never changes. Yet, today, how do we respond to his love? Do we love him in return with

---

18 See Luke 16:14-6. "The Pharisees, who loved money, heard all these things and sneered at him. And he said to them, 'You justify yourselves in the sight of others, but God knows your hearts; for what is of human esteem is an abomination in the sight of God.'"
19 See Luke 14:7. Jesus noticed how the Pharisees were "choosing the places of honor at the table."
20 Luke 23:34.
21 See Heidi Russell, *The Source of All Love* (Maryknoll, NY: Orbis Books, 2016), 163. "Jesus says yes for us when we ourselves cannot or will not."

our whole hearts[22] and desire his kingdom more than anything else?[23] Or, do we find ourselves more attracted to the promises of the secular world? Where are our hearts leading us?

The Gradual Erosion of Faith

Jesus was clear in the Gospel: We cannot love God with a divided heart. We cannot love God and mammon.[24] St. Isaac the Syrian taught that there can be no knowledge of God if our heart is filled with the world.[25] Yet, herein lies one of our greatest human struggles: surrendering our will to God's will. Somehow, we always seem to know better or want to second-guess God's providence. Our ego, filled with pride, strongly resists the teachings and examples of Jesus.

C. S. Lewis wrote, "All that we call human history…[is] the long, terrible story of man trying to find something other than God which will make him happy."[26] We see this reality beginning with the ancient Israelites, who regularly grumbled or disobeyed the will of God. One of the most notable consequences of forsaking the Lord was the Babylonian captivity, when Jerusalem and the temple were destroyed, and the people were driven from their Promised Land. The Prophet Baruch wrote:

> Hear, Israel, the commandments of life: listen, and know prudence!
>
> How is it, Israel, that you are in the land of your foes, grown old in a foreign land, defiled with the dead, counted among those destined for Hades?

---

22 See Matt. 22:37.
23 See Matt. 6:33. "Seek first the kingdom of God and his righteousness …"
24 Cf. Matt. 6:24.
25 See *The Ascetical Homilies of Saint Isaac the Syrian*, rev. 2nd ed. (Boston: Holy Transfiguration Monastery, 2011), 114. Homily 1. "God will not be persuaded to dwell in a soul together with distraction over outward things." See also St. Isaac of Nineveh, *On Ascetical Life*, trans. Mary Hansbury (Crestwood, NY: St. Vladimir's Seminary Press, 1989), 26. "No one is able is able to draw near to God without leaving the world far behind. This is virtue: emptying one's mind of the world. As long as the senses are occupied with *things*, the heart cannot stop imagining them."
26 C. S. Lewis, *Mere Christianity* (New York, NY: Macmillan, 1952), 53.

Rejoice in Hope

You have forsaken the fountain of wisdom! Had you walked in the way of God, you would have dwelt in peace.[27]

In more recent times, consider Russia. During the 19th century, there was an unprecedented spiritual renaissance that gave rise to many great saints—the Optina Elders, St. Seraphim of Sarov, St. Theophan the Recluse, and St. Ignatius Brianchaninov—to name a few. Yet in the 20th century, the Communists seized control, and through oppression and extensive reeducation, tried to root out the influences of the Church and de-sensitize the human heart to God's grace. Communism in Russia and Eastern Europe destroyed millions of people spiritually. In contrast today, we voluntarily give into such destruction. Romanian Father-Confessor Ciprian Grădinaru wrote:

> In the Communist prisons, torturers used all resources available to force prisoners to deny Christ. Nowadays, rejecting Christ is done voluntarily, as people are seduced from an early age to embrace a lifestyle that is opposite to the one to which Christ calls us. In prisons, torturers were trying to prevent every person from having any kind of privacy or moments of prayer. Nowadays, people voluntarily surrender their own privacy in favor of TV, the Internet or anything which might steal their serenity and opportunity to be alone with Christ.[28]

No matter how many efforts have been made, nothing other than God will fulfill human longing or lead to happiness. To be sure, the spiritual recession did not happen overnight. Prophetic voices such as Archbishop Fulton J. Sheen warned of the trends in the late 1940s.[29]

---

27   Baruch 3:9-13.
28   See Fr. Ciprian Grădinaru, "Afterword," in Monk Moise, *The Saint of the Prisons: Notes on the Life of Valeriu Gafencu*, trans. Monk Sava, Oaşa Monastery (Triada, 2019), 283.
29   Cf. Joseph Pronechen, "Archbishop Sheen's Warning of a Crisis in Christendom," *National Catholic Register*, online, July 29, 2018.

Rejoice in Hope

The erosion of faith was gradual, each crack in the wall scarcely observable, until we suddenly found the entire structure in danger of collapse. Archbishop Sheen wrote:

> It is characteristic of any decaying civilization that the great masses of people are unconscious of the tragedy. Only those who live by faith really know what is happening in the world ... the great masses without faith are unconscious of the destructive process going on because they have lost the vision of the heights from which they fell.[30]

Our Own Experiences

Many of us might boldly declare, "I will never abandon God." Yet, do we sometimes find ourselves like Peter, who denied Jesus? Are there times when we find ourselves diluting what is important, giving something preference over God? Think about weekend sporting events or tournaments. Do these often conflict with Sunday liturgy? How about weekday evenings? Do we share a meal together as a family and pray? Or, is it chaos as each person comes and goes from the kitchen, taking meals when convenient because of school, study, or practice? Do we justify this dilution? "It will only happen this once. I will get back to church next week. It will be okay." It is the small things that compound, drawing us further away from God and leaving us exhausted. Gradually, we find ourselves losing focus on our single most important priority, putting it off until tomorrow ... and then the next tomorrow, and the next. And rest assured, the devil delights when we are pulled away from our relationship with God. In C.S. Lewis's satire *The Screwtape Letters*, master demon Screwtape writes to his nephew and understudy, Wormwood, "Indeed, the safest road to hell is the gradual one – the gentle

---

[30] Archbishop Fulton J. Sheen made this statement in 1948. Cited by Michael Cunningham, "Living the Worthy Life: Now More Than Ever We Need Jesus Christ," *Catholic365* online (February 5, 2021).

slope, soft underfoot, without sudden turnings, without milestones, without signposts."[31]

Sometimes we delude ourselves, saying, "I am doing better than most. I go to church on Sunday. What I am doing is good enough." This is indicative of faith that is superficial, not to the depth necessary to produce fruit and gain eternal life. Our house is built on sand and when the inevitable storm comes, it will collapse.[32] Or some may be tempted to follow the crowd. Yet Jesus warns against this, saying it is the broad road that leads to destruction, and those who enter through it are many.[33] There is no safety in numbers, and following human initiative is foolish because our will is weak and wounded by sin. The only surety is following Jesus—and it is the road less traveled—because conventional wisdom tells us not to. But Jesus is unconventional. He is the light that shines in the darkness,[34] no matter how deep the gloom may seem.

Complacency is another grave danger. Many are deluded into believing we have plenty of time, yet as St. Ignatius Brianchaninov wrote, "He who sins willfully and intentionally, hoping to repent later, insidiously schemes against God. He will be struck down by an unexpected death, without the time he counted on to begin a life of virtue."[35] Jesus warned us, "Stay awake, for you know neither the day nor the hour."[36] Similarly, some are so protective of the status quo that they frantically work to accumulate treasures and possession in this world instead of cultivating the Kingdom of God within their hearts. Where do we place our priorities? We can deceive ourselves, but we cannot deceive God.

Some claim that institutionalized religion enslaves us, taking away our freedoms, and they call for liberation and embracing teachings

---

[31] C.S. Lewis, *The Screwtape Letters* (New York, NY: Harper Collins Publishing, 2000), 61. Letter XII.
[32] See Matt. 7:24-7.
[33] See Matt. 7:13.
[34] Cf. John 1:5.
[35] St. Ignatius Brianchaninov, *The Field: Cultivating Salvation*, trans. Nicholas Kotar (Jordanville, NY: Holy Trinity Monastery Publications, 2016), 172.
[36] Matt. 25:13.

that are more "politically correct." Yet, is liberated humanity happier without God? Or are we really becoming enslaved to sin? The hopelessness and disillusionment that has gripped our society gives us the answer. Despair is the opposite of hope, the consequence of abandoning the Source of Life.

God Has Not Abandoned Us

Some lament that God has abandoned us. However, has God abandoned us, or rather, have we abandoned him? God has not gone anywhere. He is always near, waiting for us. Consider the Parable of the Prodigal Son.[37] The younger son was at his lowest point in the pigpen. How far he had fallen, leaving his home, squandering his inheritance on dissolute living and prostitutes. Like him, even if we are at our lowest point, all we need to do is make that first step ("I shall get up and go to my father's house"), acknowledging our failings ("Father, I have sinned against heaven and against you"), and God will embrace us with his fatherly love ("He ran to his son, embraced him and kissed him"), welcoming us back and restoring our dignity ("Quickly … put a ring on his finger … let us celebrate with a feast"). God's love is unconditional—that is the bedrock of our faith and our source of hope.

Returning to God

When we realize we have lost our way, remember Jesus's first commandment: "Repent and believe in the Gospel."[38] He welcomes sinners and invites them to repentance with love and without severe judgment. He dined with Zacchaeus despite his notoriety, forgave the adulterous woman about to be stoned, received the repentant Mary Magdalen and opened to her the mysteries of the interior life, spoke of eternal life to the Samaritan woman in spite of her unsavory past, and promised prompt entry into heaven to the repentant thief on the

---

37 Luke 15:11-32.
38 Cf. Mark 1:15.

cross.[39] The Good Shepherd left the 99 sheep to search for the one that had strayed and, upon finding it, gently carried it back on his shoulders with great joy.[40] The Good News of the Gospel is that Jesus suffered, died, rose, and ascended into heaven for our salvation. He desires the lost to be found. He wills for those who are in danger of losing their souls to be saved. "There is great joy in heaven over the repentant,"[41] Jesus said.

However, how often do we reflect on the Good News of Jesus? Or is the voice we hear more commonly the sirens of our culture calling to us with their sweet songs filled with fantasies, illusions, and empty promises of instant happiness? And, when we become enchanted by them and follow them, we find our lives crashing against the rock of vainglory.[42] Jesus Christ is our only true hope. If we anchor our lives to anything else, it will eventually fail us.

The devil would like people to believe they are beyond the grace of God; however, the depth and fullness of God's mercy cannot be judged with human understanding, which is flawed and limited. No one is beyond the mercy of God. To think otherwise is a denial of God—blasphemy—the unpardonable sin against the Holy Spirit[43] because it is the sinner himself who prevents God from forgiving him. Further, "the devil fears a person who hopes, because he knows from experience what a greatly compassionate God we have."[44]

"Repent and believe in the Gospel." Let us humbly repent and confess our faults, failings, and the illnesses of our soul. A sincere and pure confession provides us with a reset, a true encounter with the Divine Physician, the healer of souls and bodies. It will prepare us to receive Eucharist, which strengthens our resolve to avoid those behaviors that separate us from God. Like the Prodigal, we simply

---

39 See Fr. Reginald Garrigou-LaGrange, O.P., "Understanding Our Lord's Relentless Love," *Magnificat*, 24(9) (2022), 54.
40 See Luke 15:3-7.
41 Cf. Luke 15:7.
42 See St. John Chrysostom, *On the Priesthood*, trans. Graham Neville (Crestwood, NY: St. Vladimir's Seminary Press, 1964), 76-8. He uses the image of sirens and the rock of vainglory.
43 Cf. Matt. 12:31.
44 *Counsels from the Holy Mountain*, 266.

Rejoice in Hope

need to take that first step toward the Father, and he will run to greet us with unconditional love. Rejoice in hope. What are waiting for?

Instructions for Personal Reflection

Each of us comes into this retreat at a different point on the spiritual journey. As we assess where we are, we strive to recommit ourselves to the Art of Spiritual Life. Accordingly, at the end of each conference, we will provide a short reflection. This is to be read, alone and in silence. Based on the discussion in the conference and this reflection, consider some questions that might help us assess our personal situations.

Reflection

Dorothy Day was a stubborn, headstrong woman who had a deep-seated longing for something more. Her heart was constantly searching. A journalist and social activist, she regularly marched to protest the injustices of her day. She lived a bohemian lifestyle, was an avowed atheist, and had Communist leanings. She drank, partied, became pregnant, and had an illegal abortion, afraid of losing the man who had impregnated her. He left her, anyway. In 1917, she was imprisoned in Washington, DC, for participating in a women's suffrage rally. She and her group began a hunger strike. In her autobiography, she wrote:

> I began asking for a Bible the second day I was imprisoned, and by the fourth day it was brought to me. I read it with the sense of coming back to something of my childhood that I had lost. My heart swelled with joy and thankfulness for the Psalms. The man who sang these songs knew sorrow and expected joy.
>
> I clung to the words of comfort in the Bible and as

Rejoice in Hope

long as the light held out, I read and pondered. Yet all the while I read, my pride was fighting on. I did not want to go to God in defeat and sorrow. I did not want to depend on Him. I was like the child that wants to walk by itself, I kept brushing away the hand that held me up. I tried to persuade myself that I was reading for literary enjoyment. But the words kept echoing in my heart. I prayed and I did not know that I prayed.[45]

How many times have we found ourselves like Dorothy, brushing away the invitation of Jesus, not wanting to go to him in defeat and sorrow, not wanting to give in to his presence because of stubbornness or hardness of heart? Or deep-seated pride? How often have we found ourselves praying, not knowing that we were praying? How often are we shackled by guilt for past sins? How often do we want to dictate our own terms for accepting Jesus's invitation? Dorothy's experience is common, and her search for meaning opened her heart to tremendous spiritual awakening.

True Christian living begins with a choice to follow Jesus Christ. St. Theophan the Recluse wrote:

> There is a moment, and a very noticeable moment, which is sharply marked out in the course of our life, when a person begins to live in a Christian way. Christian life is zeal and the strength to remain in communion with God by means of an active fulfillment of his holy will, according to our faith in our Lord Jesus Christ, and with the help of the grace of God, to the glory of his most holy name.
>
> The essence of Christian life consists in communion with God, in Christ Jesus our Lord—in a communion with God which in the beginning is usually hidden not

---

[45] Dorothy Day, *The Long Loneliness: The Autobiography of Dorothy Day* (San Francisco, CA: Harper, 1952), 80-1.

only from others, but also from oneself. The testimony of this life that is visible or can be felt within us is the ardor of active zeal to please God in a Christian manner, with total self-sacrifice and hatred of everything which is opposed to this. And so, when this ardor of zeal begins, Christian life has its beginning. The person in whom this ardor is constantly active is one who is living in a Christian way ....

Having a firm basis in such an understanding, one may easily conclude that a cold fulfillment of the rules of the Church just like routine in business, which is established by our calculating mind, or like correct and dignified behavior and honesty in conduct, is not a decisive indicator that the true Christian life is present in us. All this is good, but as long as it does not bear in itself the spirit of life in Christ Jesus, it has no value at all before God. Such things would then be like soulless statues. Good clocks also work correctly; but who will say that there is life in them? It is the same thing here.

This good order in one's conduct more than anything else can lead one into deception. Its true significance depends upon one's inward disposition, where it is possible that there are significant deviations from real righteousness in one's righteous deeds. Thus, while refraining outwardly from sinful deeds, one may have an attraction for them or a delight from them in one's heart; so also, doing righteous deeds outwardly, one's heart may not be in them. Only true zeal both wishes to do good in all fullness and purity, and persecutes sin in its smallest forms. It seeks the good as its daily bread, and with sin it fights as with a mortal enemy.[46]

---

[46] St. Theophan the Recluse, *The Path to Salvation: A Concise Outline of Christian Ascesis*, trans. Seraphim Rose (Stafford, AZ: St. Paisius Monastery), 23-5.

In the case of Dorothy, she converted to Catholicism and decided to follow Jesus in a radical way. With Peter Maurin, she founded the Catholic Worker Movement, a nonviolent, pacifist movement that continues to this day, combining direct aid for the poor and homeless with nonviolent direct action on their behalf. "I really only love God as much as I love the person I love the least," Dorothy wrote. She was also a strong advocate of the Universal Call to Holiness—the belief that all people are called to be holy.[47] In some retreat notes, she wrote, "There is room for greater saints now than ever before. Never has the world been so organized — press, radio, education, recreation — to turn minds away from Christ. ... We are all called to be saints."[48] Dorothy wrote these words in the early 1940s, long before the internet and current technology. Her cause for canonization has been opened.

Reflection Questions

1. What is my greatest priority in life? To what do I devote the greatest amount of time? Does this impact my relationship with God? If so, what am I willing to do about it?

2. Do I sometimes find myself like the Prodigal, in the pigpen? Do I desire to return to the Lord? What prevents me from seeking forgiveness?

3. Am I hopeful or despairing? What is the cause of my present condition?

---

[47] See Second Vatican Council, *Lumen Gentium* (November 21, 1964), Chapter V. Discusses the Universal Call to Holiness, which is based on Jesus's teaching, "Be perfect, just as your heavenly Father is perfect" (Matt. 5:48).

[48] Carl Bunderson, "Gomez Highlights Dorothy Day, Universal Call to Holiness in Final USCCB Speech," *The Pillar* (November 15, 2022).

RETREAT CONFERENCE

Endure in Affliction

"Many false prophets will arise and deceive many; and because of the increase of evildoing, the love of many will grow cold. But the one who perseveres to the end will be saved."
(Matt. 24:11-13)

"The more gold is tried in fire, the purer it becomes. And the more a Christian is tried by temptations, the more his soul is purified." [49]
(Elder Ephraim of Arizona)

"The way of living in eternity depends on the way man lived on earth."
(Patriarch Daniel of Romania)

Introduction

There is no compromise between the Gospel (joy) and the world (emptiness). There are only two ways, and we cannot follow both. This is not to say that living according to the commandments of Jesus is easy. However, rather than being constrained by human frailties, influenced by a world that endorses pursuit of sensual pleasures, vanity, or material goods, let us consider how can we fulfill the commandments of Jesus. Or, phrased another way, "How can we follow God with an undivided heart?" This is especially relevant in a world growing increasingly hostile to Gospel values.

Opening Gospel Reading:
Conditions for Following Christ

A reading from the Holy Gospel according to Luke:

---

49 *Counsels from the Holy Mountain*, 256.

> Then Jesus said to them, "If anyone wishes to come after me, he must deny himself and take up his cross daily and follow me. For whoever wishes to save his life will lose it, but whoever loses his life for my sake will save it. What profit is there for one to gain the whole world yet lose or forfeit himself? Whoever is ashamed of me and of my words, the Son of Man will be ashamed of when he comes in his glory and in the glory of the Father and of the holy angels."[50]

The Gospel of the Lord.

The Cross is the Way to Salvation

Welcome to the arena! Once we have made a firm decision to follow Christ, we consent to a constant state of warfare until our last breath.[51] The devil will do anything possible to upend our relationship with the Divine. Elder Ephraim of Arizona said:

> Just as the athlete is tested in the arena and in the field of action, likewise the Christian is tested in the arena of struggles as to whether he truly loves God. Patience in the struggle against various sins and courage at their onset to apply the divine commandments characterize the fervent worshipper of Christ.[52]

Jesus is unequivocally clear. His way is the way of the cross, which we as disciples must also shoulder. For many, this is where Christianity hits a speedbump—who wants a simple inconvenience, much less a cross? Perseverance is required, and some grow weary from the effort, concluding it's just too hard, especially when there are so many other attractive offers that require far less effort. For example, there are many who prefer the "prosperity gospel"—the narrative

---

50 Luke 9:23-6.
51 *Counsels from the Holy Mountain*, 275. "The struggle is not small; it does not last for only one day, but until our last breath."
52 Ibid., 413.

that makes many appealing promises.[53] Yet, this is not the Gospel of Jesus—actually quite the opposite because it aligns with the Pharisaic way of thinking to which Jesus took exception. Yet, many choose an easier path, separating themselves from the Truth and the Source of Life. And remember, the absence of life is death.

German Pastor and Theologian Dietrich Bonhoeffer described this phenomenon well, comparing cheap grace versus costly grace:

> Cheap grace is the preaching of forgiveness without repentance, baptism without church discipline, Communion without confession, absolution without personal confession. Cheap grace is grace without discipleship, grace without the cross, grace without Jesus Christ, living and incarnate.[54]

This is the way the world today tries to mold Christianity, to accommodate the spirit of the age, trying to eliminate the Cross. "Christianity would be so much easier if only …" Thus, the secular world tries to devalue the importance of the Gospel. To this, Bonhoeffer contrasts the true cost of discipleship:

> Costly grace is the gospel which must be *sought* again and again, the gift which must be *asked for*, the door at which a man must *knock*. Such grace is *costly* because it causes us to follow, and it is *grace* because it calls us to follow *Jesus Christ*. It is costly because it costs a man his life, and it is grace because it gives a man the only true life. It is costly because it condemns

---

[53] See Mark J. Cartledge, "Liberation Theology Opted for the Poor, and the Poor Opted for [Neo-] Pentecostalism—Illustrating the Influence of the 'Prosperity Gospel' in Brazil," *International Academy of Practical Theology*, Conference Series (2021). Brazil was originally an overwhelmingly Catholic country which has shifted to one of the largest Pentecostal populations in the world, and where Catholics will be less than 50% of the population by 2025. "One of the main reasons it appears that people are attracted to the prosperity gospel is because of the hope it gives people: there is a way out of poverty and lives can change for the better" (85).

[54] Dietrich Bonhoeffer, *The Cost of Discipleship* (New York, NY: Simon & Schuster, 1995), 44-5.

sin, and grace because it justifies the sinner. Above all, it is *costly* because it cost God the life of his Son.[55]

Following Jesus on the path to eternal life has a cost, obedience to the divine will[56] and humility, realizing we cannot achieve our salvation on our own. The Christian faith must be lived authentically, staying the course, and not trying to seek an easier way that is free of struggle. The trials we endure are for the greater benefit of our souls, preparation to receive even greater blessings.[57] Elder Ephraim of Arizona succinctly states:

> Is there anyone who has entered by paradise by a different path, a path without temptations, whom we can imitate? No. all the saints passed through fire and water, through various temptations and afflictions, and they glorified God with their patience and received crowns of eternal glory.[58]

Similarly, St. Isaac the Syrian wrote that if the soul does not consciously share in the sufferings of Christ, she will never have communion with him.[59] And only by being united to our Savior can he lead us to heaven.

Watchfulness (Being Constantly on Guard)

Many of the Holy Fathers speak to us about watchfulness

---

55 Ibid., 45.
56 See *Counsels from the Holy Mountain*, 9. "Since we desire to live a Christ-like life, we obliged to submit to God's will, because all things come from God. And they are from God—and thus are the divine will—the Heavenly Father commands them. Shall we not obey?"
57 Ibid., 28. "Have patience, my child, in the trial which the goodness of God is sending you for the greater benefit of your soul. You should rejoice, because this shows God's concern for your greater spiritual progress, primarily in humility. Many times, man's pride becomes a cause for God to give a fatherly 'slap' so that we walk more securely in humility. This is the best sign of how greatly God is concerned for our souls."
58 Ibid., 254.
59 *The Ascetical Homilies of Saint Isaac* the Syrian, Homily Five, 160. "If the soul does not taste Christ's sufferings consciously, she will never have communion with him."

(*nepsis*).[60] They advise us that once the heart and soul have been swept clean through sacramental Confession and strengthened by the Eucharist, the Presence of Christ within, we must remain ever-vigilant as to thoughts that may wish to breach our minds, create temptation, and draw us away from God. A single demon slipping through a crack will lead to another, and then another, and can we can quickly find ourselves overwhelmed. To be clear, the devil can only make suggestions; we must act on them, thereby being led into sin.[61] Therefore, it is important to cut off the thought before it becomes implanted. Or, as St. Paisios of Mount Athos said, "If you see a thought flying like a helicopter and trying to land where it shouldn't—in other words, a persistent thought—then you take the bazooka and boom! –Then confess it."[62]

Elder Ephraim warns, "If we love ourselves more than God, we will tend towards sin."[63] There are a number of reasons we can be led astray and we need to remain conscious of breaches.

First is our pride and ego. Pride caused Adam to fall; he desired to be like God instead of dependent on him. St. Ignatius Brianchaninov, referencing St. Macarius the Great, wrote, "Even the purest and most perfect human being has in himself a grain of pride."[64] The Holy Fathers had much to say about this passion. St. John Climacus wrote: "Pride is utter poverty of the soul disguised as riches, imaginary light where in fact there is darkness,"[65] and added, "Like a worm in

---

60 In many works, the Philokalic Fathers are referred to as the "Watchful Fathers." *Nepsis* can be translated as watchfulness, vigilance, or attentiveness.
61 See Ioanichie Balan, *Elder Cleopa of Sihastria in the Tradition of St. Paisius Velichkovsky*, trans. Mother Cassina (Lake George, CO: New Varatec Publishing, 2001), 160. Elder Cleopa said, "If someone wants to sin, he sins; if he does not want to sin, he doesn't. The Devil only puts the ideas in our minds, so if someone is foolish and deceived, he commits the sin."
62 "St. Paisios the Athonite on Spiritual Warfare," *The Ascetic Experience* online (Sept. 28, 2019). https://www.asceticexperience.com.
63 *Counsels from the Holy Mountain*, 188.
64 St. Ignatius Brianchaninov, *The Field: Cultivating Salvation*, trans. Nicholas Kotar (Jordanville, NY: Holy Trinity Monastery Publications, 2016), 187. See also Pseudo-Macarius, *The Fifty Spiritual Homilies and the Great Letter*, trans. George A. Maloney, SJ (New York, NY: Paulist Press, 1992), 80. "Indeed, even a pure nature also has in itself a certain amount of pride."
65 Ibid., 209-10.

a tree this unholy enemy gnaws away all hope."[66] Pride has many manifestations, including vainglory, vanity, selfishness, arrogance, self-confidence, anger, irritability, grumbling, self-pity, discontent, an insatiable desire for more, ingratitude, malice, judgment, self-justification, lack of accountability, impatience, and mercilessness.

Second is our predisposition toward sin. We may have an ingrained sinful habit and, even though we have confessed our failings, we remain vulnerable; the temptor will test us to see if we will fall into this same sin again. We need to work hard to change our previous default settings and ways of behaving. Without a deliberate effort to avoid occasions of a particular sin, we will likely stumble. Thus, we may need to change our friends,[67] how spend our free time, the books we read, the television shows or movies we watch, the music to which we listen, or other facets of our lives in order to avoid that which could lead us into sin.

Third, by being made in the image of God, we were created with imagination. Elder Ephraim said, "All the evil begins when a person gives into his imagination and allows sinful thoughts to prevail." Through a subtle breach, the devil can introduce a thought, which may appear delightful and innocent. If we detect this encroachment early and dismiss it, then we avoid sin. However, left unchecked, the thought can grow stronger and we can be ensnared by it. This can further deepen to obsession: the injured person thinks about getting revenge, the drunkard thinks about his next drink, the fornicator obsesses about a particular woman, the worrisome person becomes concerned with money, and so on.[68] Such escalation becomes sinful[69] and can lead to even more serious sins. The sooner we can hit this thought with the bazooka, the better. Elder Ephraim warns:

---

66 Ibid., 211.
67 Cf. *The Priestmonk Eusebius Giannakakis*, trans. Fr. Peter A. Chambera (Montréal, QC: Alexander Press, 2021), 173. "Keep yourself far from disorderly and careless people, avoid becoming conformed to them, for this is the greatest enemy of the spiritual life."
68 See Sergius Bolshakoff and M. Basil Pennington, OCSO, *In Search of True Wisdom: Visits to Eastern Spiritual Fathers* (New York, NY: Alba House, 1979), 31.
69 See Matt. 5:27-8. ""You have heard that it was said, 'You shall not commit adultery.' But I say to you, everyone who looks at a woman with lust has already committed adultery with her in his heart."

> Just as you avoid fire so that you do not get burned, and a snake so that you do not get bitten, likewise—and even more so—you should avoid the devil's fantasies! Be careful, I repeat, with filthy fantasies, because is how great spiritual men have fallen and perished ….
>
> Drive evil thoughts away quickly—kick them out! Shout, 'Get out of here, you tramps, out of the temple of God, out of my soul!'[70]

We might be tempted to dismiss our thoughts—thoughts are harmless, or so we may think. Yet the demons will continuously try to breach our defenses through suggestions and memories of the past; they are relentless, and we are weak. We have volumes of memories in picture books stored within our minds, so there is plenty of source material from which the demons can provide appealing suggestions. Addictions or previous sinful behaviors further increase our vulnerability to an attack. We can get carried away with pleasant thoughts, reminiscing, all too comfortable, like visiting an old friend. Coupled with a secular society that embraces individualistic behaviors and immoral lifestyles—*it's okay, don't worry about it*—the risk of giving into temptation is ever greater. We need to be constantly vigilant. Elder Eusebius Giannakakis asked his spiritual children, "Do we have an obligation to certain thoughts? Are we required to receive them, to offer them coffee and pastry, and provide them with hospitality?" "No!," he would firmly say. "It is not worth it."[71]

Elder Ephraim noted, "The mind is an area, a place. If God does not occupy it, then the enemy will."[72] He further advises, "We should always strive to have salvific thoughts and beneficial images in our mind, so that we do not leave room for Satan to throw in his garbage—sinful thoughts and fantasies."[73]

---

70   *Counsel from the Holy Mountain*, 282.
71   Cf. *The Priestmonk Eusebius Giannakakis*, 327.
72   Cf. *Counsels from the Holy Mountain*, 370.
73   Ibid.

Striving for Holiness (Our Universal Call)

We are called to be holy,[74] yet great struggle is required to achieve our exalted goal of life in heaven. What tangible steps can take to fill our hearts with Christ and avoid becoming a dumping ground for the devil's garbage? Let us consider three spiritual supports that can be used to combat pride and temptation, strengthening us for the struggle against secularizing influences. These will aid in building the interior life and fortifying one's faith: (1) the Divine Liturgy and sacramental life of the Church, (2) the Jesus Prayer, and (3) Philokalic reading.[75]

Divine Liturgy – is at the center of Eastern Christian spiritual life (Catholic and Orthodox), and it is intended to be a dynamic encounter, combining both heaven and earth in worship of the Triune God. It is the whole summation of our belief, the highpoint of encounter through the Eucharist. Holy Communion is mystical communion with the God-Man Jesus Christ. It is intended to be a transcendent experience, dramatic, deeply moving, and a spiritual action that lifts up the soul. Patriarch Daniel (Ciobotea) of Romania wrote, "The Divine Liturgy constitutes the most profound vision of God as a mystery of love and communion ..."[76] In the liturgy, we are filled with reverence, awe, emotion, and great awareness of the sacred things being celebrated. We stand before the Holy Table with fear and trembling, captured in a sacred reality, reminding us of our true destiny of union with God in the company of his angels and his saints. Elder Eusebius said:

> There is no other gift on earth that is greater, more

---

74 See Matt. 5:48. "Be perfect, just as your heavenly Father is perfect." Universal Call to Holiness.
75 See Aurelian Iftimiu, "Patriarch Daniel Offers Remedy for Secularization during Bucharest Monastic Synaxis," *Basilica News Agency*, online (Nov. 28, 2022). The remedy to secularization is "increased prayer (hesychast prayer), a return to the Holy Fathers and their works, and an intensification of communion." These have been at the core of the spiritual renewal in the Romanian Church.
76 Patriarch Daniel, "The One Church and the Many Churches," in *Rebuilding Orthodoxy in Romania,* ed. Chad Hatfield (Yonkers, NY: St. Vladimir's Seminary Press, 2021), 47.

precious, and more holy than that of the divine worship and the Cup of Life. This is what gives us peace ... what unites us with our Lord, our sweetest Jesus. He instructed his spiritual children according to the Apostolic and Patristic tradition and cultivated their soul, so that they could participate frequently in the Mystery of Holy Eucharist, knowing well that the medicine of immortality is Holy Communion, the secret of holiness and the engagement of the future kingdom of God. In one of homilies in church, Fr. Eusebius said ...

'I think that our life, if it is not fortified and if it does not partake continually of the great Banquet of Life, it remains empty. It remains seriously deprived and impoverished. Our faith must be a living, a practicing faith. We must not easily set aside and exclude the Divine Liturgy from our life. We must not easily abstain from the Cup of Life, which is the ultimate gift of life.'[77]

Elder Eusebius adds, "Christ, whom we receive each time, should not merely warm us, but should create a fire in us to burn away evil and sin. We offer hospitality to the Lord of heaven and earth in our soul."[78] The Elder also advocated more frequent reception of Holy Communion.[79] Others who had similar perspectives were St. Basil the

---

77 *The Priestmonk Eusebius Giannakakis*, 195-6.
78 Ibid., 250.
79 Ibid., 195. "He instructed his spiritual children according to the Apostolic and Patristic tradition and cultivated their soul, so they could participate frequently in the Mystery of Holy Eucharist, knowing well that the medicine for immortality is Holy Communion, the secret of holiness and the engagement of the future kingdom of God."

Great,[80] the Kollyvades Fathers,[81] and St. John of Kronstadt.[82]

Of course, to enter more deeply into the liturgy, proper preparation is required. This includes sacramental Confession, preparing ourselves to be filled with the presence of Christ. Elder Eusebius advised, "For one to reach the Cup of Life, one must first go through the process of repentance, confession, the study of Sacred Scripture, and the holy struggle against all those things that are against the will of God."[83] And he emphasized, "A sincere and pure confession is the best preparation for the Mystery of Holy Eucharist."[84]

Preparation should also include fasting. Elder Ephraim explains:

> Fasting is not just abstention from food, but primarily strict abstinence of the senses. When the senses are fed by external things, they transmit a corresponding amount of poison to the *nous*[85] and the heart, which kills the soul's life in God. Our Watchful Fathers[86] have so much to tell us about holy fasting of the senses. Their entire teaching is mainly directed at the purification of the *nous* from sinful fantasies and thoughts, and the purification of the heart from feelings that defile it.

---

80 Ibid., 249. "St. Basil the Great had the rule of receiving Holy Communion four times a week." Sunday, Wednesday, Friday, and Saturday.
81 Ibid., 309. "Fr. Eusebius struggled to dissolve the superstition around the issue of receiving Holy Communion frequently. He always emphasized the necessity but also the presuppositions for frequent participation in the Mystery of the Holy Eucharist." He said, "When one communes more frequently, one is thus blessed and motivated to be more careful and to avoid mistakes." See also St. Nikodimos the Hagiorite, *Concerning Frequent Communion of the Immaculate Mysteries of Christ*, trans. George Dokos (Thessaloniki, Greece: Uncut Mountain Press, 2006), 122. "When he begins to think about the act that he will be receiving Communion again in just a few days, he doubles his efforts to watch over himself .... This is because he is pressed on two sides: on one side, because just a short while ago he received Communion, and on the other, because he will receive again in just a short while." Note that St. Nikodimos was a Kollyvades Father.
82 See Philip Sheldrake, *Spirituality: A Brief History*, 2nd ed. (West Sussex, UK: Wiley-Blackwell, 2013), 196. Per Sheldrake, one of three important features of St. John of Kronstadt's spirituality was daily Eucharist is central.
83 *The Priestmonk Eusebius Giannakakis*, 309.
84 Ibid., 311.
85 *Nous* – defined by the Holy Fathers as the rational part of the soul. That which pertains to the *nous* is "noetic" (adj.), and the Jesus Prayer is often called "noetic prayer."
86 Watchful Fathers is another term used for the Philokalic Fathers.

> Furthermore, they teach teach that we must eradicate every evil in its beginning to keep the soul clean.[87]

Full engagement is required to experience heaven on earth and celebrate the liturgy as it is intended. This means properly preparing to participate in the Mystery of Holy Eucharist.

Jesus Prayer – Filling our hearts with love of God means removing the clutter that has accumulated through the pursuit of worldly things and the trash the devil wishes to deposit there. Patriarch Daniel wrote, "The first and ultimate source of love, of true joy and true peace, is *prayer*. Nothing in this world can replace prayer. Therefore, prayer as communion with God is the life of the Christian soul."[88] He also wrote, "True theology is always born out of the life of the Church that prays, confesses, and serves."[89] Whereas the liturgy is communal, the Jesus Prayer is what binds us individually with God in a deeply personal, intimate relationship; in turn, intensifying the liturgical experience.

Philokalic Reading – like industrious bees, we gather the spiritual honey from the teachings of the Holy Fathers, who have much to say about following the commandments of Jesus. The idea of Philokalic reading is not just returning to the Fathers; it is an effort to gain a deeper grasp of their spirit.[90] Today, with spiritual fathers being fewer in number, the writings can provide us with ongoing guidance. "If we pay careful attention to these writings as if it were to those Fathers themselves, by reading them with Fear of God and understanding, and with God's help, we can become imitators of their God-pleasing life."[91] Elder Eusebius challenged those under his spiritual guidance saying:

---

[87] *Counsels from the Holy Mountain*, 279.
[88] Patriarch Daniel, *Confessing the Truth in Love: Orthodox Perceptions of Life, Mission and Unity*, 2nd ed. (Bucharest, RO: Basilica, 2008), 106.
[89] Patriarch Daniel, "The Unity between Theology and Spirituality," in *Rebuilding Orthodoxy in Romania*, 20.
[90] Cf. Patriarch Daniel, *Confessing the Truth in Love*, 127.
[91] Cf. Fr. Clement Sederholm, *Elder Leonid of Optina*, "The Optina Elders Series," vol. 1, trans. from Russian (Platina, CA: St. Herman of Alaska Brotherhood, 2002), 49.

Rejoice in Hope

> Do you want to be a saint? Do you want to be angelic? Enter into the mind and spirit of the Holy Fathers of the Church, embrace their spirit, and close within your thought and heart the life of the ascetics, the life of the Fathers, who have shown so brightly.[92]

Like Holy Confession being a preparation for receiving Holy Eucharist, the study of scripture is an important requisite for reading the Holy Fathers. Elder Eusebius noted, "Sacred Scripture is truly a gold mine ... that is unique and incomparable. It is from there that the Fathers drew their inspiration."[93] Let us connect with the Holy Fathers, and identify one as a spiritual guide for our own journey.

The Three Spiritual Supports – the Divine Liturgy, the Jesus Prayer, and the writings of the Philokalic Fathers—can help fill our hearts and minds with Christ and drive out all that is of the devil and the world. This will allow us to grow rich in what matters to God: love, humility, mercy, compassion, obedience, patient endurance, and long-suffering—to name a few—treasures that cannot be stolen nor decay and will allow us to thrive during spiritual recession.

Endure in Affliction

Jesus told us that his is the way of the Cross. He was unambiguous.[94] St. Isaac the Syrian wrote:

> The path of God is a daily cross. No one has ascended into heaven by means of ease, for we know where the way of ease leads, and how it ends. God never wishes the man who gives himself up to him with his whole heart to be without concern (that is, concern over the truth). But from this he knows that he is under God's providence—that he perpetually sends him griefs.[95]

---

92 *The Priestmonk Eusebius Giannakakis*, 251.
93 Ibid.
94 Cf. Luke 9:23.
95 *The Ascetical Homilies of St. Isaac the Syrian*, 430. Homily 59.

Endure in Affliction

We cannot get to heaven without the cross. Elder Ephraim summarized this well:

> Each of us bears a cross in accordance with his strength, in order that we all may resemble Christ, who in his life on earth, also bore the cross for our sake. So if we suffer together with our Christ, only then will we also be glorified together with him.[96]

Living Jesus's commandments requires constant perseverance, which in turn attracts grace granted by God as gift to those who are willing to struggle.[97] Elder Eusebius wrote, "I know, my child, that the cross you are carrying is heavy. But look to Christ the Bridegroom ... From him you will draw patience."[98] Elder Ephraim adds, "If you want to be a child of God, endure the afflictions and trials sent by God with thanksgiving, faith, and hope."[99] This is the way shown to us by Jesus himself.

Elder Ephraim also reminds us,

> It is impossible for a person to proceed without ever stumbling somewhere, because from all sides the devil, the world, and the flesh are continuously inserting obstacles into his life, and he stumbles in proportion to his carelessness.[100]

Every step of our lives must be ordered toward repentance followed by watchfulness. Repentance helps transfigure humans in their desire to be united to God. Further, we have three spiritual supports to strengthen us against stumbling: the Divine Liturgy, the Jesus Prayer, and writings of the Philokalic Fathers who teach us how

---

[96] *Counsels from the Holy Mountain*, 272.
[97] Cf. 1 Cor. 10:13. "God is faithful and will not let you be tried beyond your strength; but with the trial he will also provide a way out, so that you may be able to bear it."
[98] *The Priestmonk Eusebius Giannakakis*, 346.
[99] *Counsels of the Holy Mountain*, 10.
[100] Ibid., 130.

to live the commandments of Jesus. While the struggle is not easy, we can continuously strive to grow in holiness and thwart the assaults of the demons. We begin with incremental steps, following the guidance of those who have gone before us, and then relying on God's grace to sustain us in battle. Elder Eusebius said:

> The holy can grow holier! This is the goal and aim for all of us ... to grow spiritually and increase in holiness. We are not to remain static ... the greatest asset, the most essential, the strongest for our way of life is holiness.[101] Effort is what is important to God; 'the important thing is not to lose our immortal life, the life without end.'[102]

"Struggle, my children, struggle," encourages Elder Ephraim. "No matter how much the enemy fights against you, take courage and we shall overcome him. We have Christ, the Commander-in-Chief, who said, 'I have overcome the world.'"[103] Life here is temporary; eternity awaits in the future life.[104] And the three spiritual supports can aid us on the journey. "May God make us worthy to accept thankfully whatever he sends our way, either good or unpleasant ..."[105]

Reflection

In his teenage years, Valeriu Gafencu joined the Legion of St. Michael, a Romanian organization of a mystical and religious character. It focused on traditional Romanian values including the Orthodox faith, standing against corrupting influences such as Free Masonry. Although personally opposed to violence, certain

---

101 *The Priestmonk Eusebius Giannakakis*, 255.
102 Ibid., 150.
103 *Counsels from the Holy Mountain*, 255.
104 See *The Priestmonk Eusebius Giannakakis*, 146.
105 Ibid., 404.

elements of the Legion were more radical, causing the government to imprison many. Valeriu was incarcerated at age 20, first by the Romanian government, and later by the Communists. He spent his entire adult a life in prison, suffering greatly and eventually dying in Târgu Ocna, bedridden in a prison ward for the terminally ill, suffering from tuberculosis. With other prisoners, he dedicated himself to the ascetical life, reading of the *Philokalia*, and the Jesus Prayer, contributing to the birth of Philokalic spirituality in Communist prisons (an "Ascetic of Aiud Prison"). Equating his prison cell to a monastic cell, he encouraged fellow prisoners to spiritual purification and renewal through his sacrificial love and constant spiritual struggle, and he attained significant spiritual heights. He is considered a modern-day Romanian confessor, even though he was a layperson. He was declared a "Saint of the Prisons" by theologian Fr. Nicolae Steinhardt for "exemplary Christian conduct and devotion to those in suffering." There were many conversion stories attributed to his witness. Alexandr Solzhenitsyn wrote about his own experience in Communist prisons:

> Bless you prison, bless you for being in my life. For there, lying upon the rotting prison straw, I came to realize that the object of life is not prosperity as we are made to believe, but the maturity of the human soul.[106]

Valeriu's attitude was similar, and he exemplifies endurance in affliction, having suffered much, yet always striving to grow closer to Christ through prayer and spiritual reading.[107] He participated in the Holy Mysteries of Confession and Holy Eucharist, received spiritual

---

106 Alexandr Solzhenitsyn, *The Gulag Archipelago*. This sentiment summarizes well the perspective of Gafencu.
107 Valeriu Gafencu was able to read the first four volumes of the *Philokalia* that had been translated by Fr. Dumitru Stăniloae into Romanian. This would ultimately become a 12-volume work. Gafencu and others had greater access to spiritual writings, to priests, and the Sacraments when imprisoned by the Romanian government prior to Communism, where there was greater appreciation for human rights. This significantly changed under the Communists when the focus was placed on reeducation.

Rejoice in Hope

guidance when a priest was available, with other dedicated prisoners he developed a prayer schedule for ongoing prayer day and night, and significantly encouraged others in their suffering. In a 1942 letter, he wrote, "In life faith is everything. Without it a man is like dead." He also said, "The Church and its role as an institution integrates the world into Christ. It is not concerned with only a part of life but all of life."[108]

If my life were in constant turmoil, imprisoned without hope of release, could I endure the struggle? Would I make my relationship with God a priority? Would I give thanks to God in all things? Could I deprive myself, sharing my food or medicine with those who were hungry or ill? How important would my faith be? What would I do to survive?

Consider the spiritual counsel of Elder Eusebius:

> What is needed? Will. And with the will comes the struggle. 'I want to go to Paradise. I want to become a saint. I want to succeed in my initial effort ...' From now on we must hold Paradise in our hands, and not simply be asking, 'Are we going to Paradise?' Why then did we begin (the spiritual journey)? One may say, 'I have negligence, laziness, disorderliness.' None of that! Everything will be discarded with the grace of God. Is the Lord not the almighty? Have we not started going to him, are we not committed to him? We abandon all and embrace Christ. We walk, we offer ourselves, we work, we struggle for Christ ...

> We must all become worthy of our calling and our ideal, for there is no more beautiful calling in life. It is the height, the peak .... The life of heaven is a little costly. Is it not right and just for a dedicated person to struggle to attain it?[109]

---

[108] Monk Moise, *The Saint of the Prisons: Notes on the Life of Valeriu Gafencu*, trans. Monk Sava, Oaşa Monastery (Triada, 2019), 230.
[109] *The Priestmonk Eusebius Giannakakis*, 253.

Reflection Questions

1. What struggles do I face? Do I embrace them in faith and thanksgiving as Christ's cross for me to benefit my soul? Or do I grumble against God and others?

2. How do I find encouragement to endure times of difficulty?

3. In times of challenge or struggle, do I easily give into despair? Am I often overwhelmed?

4. What practical actions can I take to empty my heart of the influences of secular culture and be filled more with Christ? Do I take advantage of the three spiritual supports we discussed: Divine Liturgy, the Jesus Prayer, and the writings of the Philokalic Fathers?

5. How do I react to the disappointments, insults, hurts, injustices, and challenges that I experience? Do I find that God is trying to tell me something? Do I discover these are also times when God provides me with his grace to endure whatever I am facing? How willingly do I accept God's perfect plan in God's perfect time?

RETREAT CONFERENCE

Persevere in Prayer

"Jesus departed to the mountain to pray, and he spent the night in prayer to God."
(Luke 6:12)

"Never neglect your prayer. The best missionary work is the one upon yourself. From there, we must begin ..." [110]
(Elder Eusebius Giannakakis)

"What is there that blessed prayer cannot set aright and renew!" [111]
(Elder Ephraim of Arizona)

Introduction

In our previous conference, we discussed the spiritual supports that aid us in our struggles: the Divine Liturgy, the Jesus Prayer, and the writings of the Philokalic Fathers. In this conference, we will delve more into the Jesus Prayer as a means of perseverance.

Opening Gospel Passage: Pray Without Becoming Weary

A reading from the Holy Gospel according to Luke:

> Jesus told his disciples a parable about the necessity for them to pray always without becoming weary. He said, "There was a judge in a certain town who neither feared God nor respected any human being. And a widow in that town used to come to him and say, 'Render a just decision for me against my adversary.' For a long time the judge was unwilling, but eventually

---

110 *The Priestmonk Eusebius Giannakakis*, 179.
111 *Counsels from the Holy Mountain*, 298.

Rejoice in Hope

he thought, 'While it is true that I neither fear God nor respect any human being, because this widow keeps bothering me I shall deliver a just decision for her lest she finally come and strike me.'"

The Lord said, "Pay attention to what the dishonest judge says. Will not God then secure the rights of his chosen ones who call out to him day and night? Will he be slow to answer them? I tell you, he will see to it that justice is done for them speedily.

"But when the Son of Man comes, will he find faith on earth?"[112]

The Gospel of the Lord.

Calling on the Sweet Name of Jesus

"In spiritual warfare, by prayer you put your battle-axe into God's hand, that he should fight your enemies and overcome them."[113] Elder Ephraim of Arizona advised, "A person's salvation depends on prayer, for this is what unites him with God and brings him near to God."[114] Prayer will "drive out despair, hopelessness, negligence, and laziness, because it will produce a new resolve, a fresh desire for new struggles."[115] Once these and other secular influences are pushed out, a person's heart can be filled with Christ. So, "say the sanctifying and salvific Jesus Prayer, and hurl yourself into the fire of the battle."[116]

In the Gospel, we regulary read how Jesus withdrew to spend time with his Father in prayer. He instructed his disciples how to pray: "Go to your inner room, close the door, and pray to your Father in

---

112 Luke 18:1-8.
113 *Unseen Warfare: Being the Spiritual Combat and Path to Paradise of Lorenzo Scupoli*, ed. Nicodemus of the Holy Mountain, rev. Theophan the Recluse, trans. E. Kadloubovsky and G. E. H. Palmer (London: Faber and Faber, 1963), 144.
114 *Counsels from the Holy Mountain*, 301.
115 Ibid., 347.
116 Ibid., 203.

Persevere in Prayer

secret. And your Father who sees in secret will repay you."[117] In our Gospel reading, we heard Jesus explain the importance of persevering in prayer and not growing weary. And in the Garden of Gethsemane, Jesus told his apostles, "Watch and pray that you may not undergo the test."[118] It is clear from Jesus's teachings and personal example that prayer is important in our faith journey and that it can provide us incredible strength to endure. ("Yet, not as I will, but as you will."[119])

Let us first consider that Jesus wants to have a deep, abiding relationship with us—not superficial, distant, cold, or abstract. He desires to draw us to himself to lead us to heaven. Similarly, each person deeply longs for relationship and, being made in the image of God, longs for God consciously or unconsciously. Prayer is one means in which we forge an enduring relationship, a person-to-person relationship, surrendering ourselves to his will and trusting that he will get us to our destiny. This elevation of the soul to touch the living God allows us to discover and experience God[120] in the eternal silence where he abides.[121] Robert Cardinal Sarah wrote, "I would say that, for a Christian, faith is man's total and absolute confidence in a God whom he has *encountered personally*."[122] It is the relational aspect that animates faith and what makes it relevant.

In this time of spiritual recession, we observe faith growing cold and one of the primary reasons is that we have lost the relational element.[123] Our relationship with God is increasingly superficial and, not perceiving the need, it is easy to drift away and seek the meaning

---

117 Matt 6:6.
118 Matt. 26:41.
119 Matt. 26:39.
120 Raya. Taken from "Faith and Prayer, *Magnificat*, 24(9) (2022), 163.
121 Cf. Robert Cardinal Sarah, in conversation with Nicolas Diat, *The Power of Silence: Against the Dictatorship of Noise*, trans. Michael J. Miller (San Francisco, CA: Ignatius Press, 2017), 21. "We encounter God only in the eternal silence in which he abides."
122 Robert Cardinal Sarah, in conversation with Nicolas Diat, *The Day is Now Far Spent*, trans. Michael J. Miller (San Francisco, CA: Ignatius Press, 2019), 24. Emphasis added by author.
123 See Gabriel Bunge, OSB, *Earthen Vessels: The Practice of Personal Prayer According to the Patristic Tradition* (San Francisco: Ignatius Press, 2002), 9. This Swiss monk describes the "evaporation of faith", and his premise is that somehow, we have lost touch with the importance of a personal prayer life which was always an essential part of the mystical tradition of the Early Church.

Rejoice in Hope

of life through other means or in other places. Elder Ephraim ascribes this being "due to our poor prayer," which, in turn, prevents us from understanding the will of God and why we "shipwreck constantly."[124] He also notes "what tempests and shipwrecks are suffered by those who rely on themselves because of their egotism."[125]

To survive and thrive in this recession, we need to rediscover the essential practice of prayer, to proactively deepen our relationship with Christ, and to stop relying on our own merits, striving to go it alone (*Don't worry, God, I've got this*). Rather, we need to follow him. Without Christ as our guide, we are heading toward spiritual bankruptcy—and certainly not heaven. Seeing the urgency of reconnecting people with prayer, especially after the global pandemic, Patriarch Daniel of Romania declared 2022 as a Solemn Year of Prayer, designating three hesychast saints as the country's patrons during this time. "Without prayer there is no Church and no Christian life … Nothing can replace prayer,"[126] he said. "Prayer is a source of joy and spiritual strength, a source of peace and love for God and for our neighbors. It is, as the holy ascetics said, 'the spiritual breath of the soul.'"[127]

This need for prayer is not just saying morning or evening prayer; it is about a complete reorientation of our lives. In doing so, we regularly turn our minds to God throughout the day, grateful for every small blessing. And during times of challenge, we turn to the Lord and ask for his mercy—and to *stop* relying on ourselves. Make a good beginning, cry out to Jesus, and seek to reap the rewards of eternal life.

Elder Ephraim often calls prayer "the sword of the Spirit."[128] We are to use it when encounter temptations or difficulties. Like Peter walking on the water and beginning to sink, prayer is the means by which we can cry out to the Lord and seek his assistance. "Lord, save

---

124 *Counsels from the Holy Mountain*, 103-4.
125 Ibid., 104.
126 Aurelian Iftimiu, "Patriarch Daniel Proclaims 2022 Solemn Year of Prayer, Commemorative Year of Hesychast Saints," *Basilica News Agency*, online (Jan. 1, 2022).
127 Ibid.
128 See *Counsels from the Holy Mountain*, 281, 291.

me!" "Lord, help me!" "Lord Jesus Christ, Son of God, have mercy on me." "Thy will be done!"

Specifically, Patriarch Daniel and the Holy Fathers speak of the importance of the Jesus Prayer, and how all walks of life—not just monks—can benefit from it. This is the oldest form of contemplative prayer in the Church, practiced and preserved in the Christian East for generations. Some say the prayer was given by Jesus himself. It emerges in the earliest traditions of the second and third centuries in which monks sought silence and solitude in the deserts of Egypt. It is referred to as hesychast prayer, Prayer of the Heart, noetic prayer, or simply *the* prayer. The purpose of this prayer is to deepen our relationship with Jesus Christ, to experience him in a profound way, and be strengthened to follow his holy will to secure our heavenly goal. Cardinal Sarah noted, "Without the nourishment of prayer, every Christian is in danger. Without the Son of God, [humans] are lost and humanity has no more future."[129] He goes on to say, "In an age that no longer prays, life turns into a rat race."[130] Thus, the urgency of returning to the regular practice of prayer, especially one that comes from the depth of one's heart, cannot be understated.

Cultivating prayer is not something new. Already in the fourth century, St. John Chrysostom wrote:

> A Christian when he eats, drinks, walks, sits, travels or does any other thing must continually cry: 'Lord Jesus Christ, Son of God, have mercy upon me.' So that the name of the Lord Jesus descending into the depths of the heart, should subdue the serpent ruling over the inner pastures and bring life and salvation to the soul.[131]

Want to avoid the occasions of sin? Pray! Want peace and tranquility in the midst of adversity? Pray! Want to reach heaven?

---
[129] Robert Cardinal Sarah, *God or Nothing: A Conversation on Faith*, trans. Michael J. Miller (San Francisco, CA: Ignatius Press, 2015), 120, 158.
[130] Ibid., 150.
[131] St. John Chrysostom. Posted by Philokalia Ministries to Facebook, November 2022.

Rejoice in Hope

Pray! Stop listening to the enemy. Pray! Do the messages of our secular culture sound appealing? Pray! "Prayer is the catapult against the demons, against the passions, against sin, and in general against everything that opposes us on the road to salvation."[132]

Remember our discussion on imagination and how this can cause us to sin? Consider the advice of Elder Ephraim:

> Do thoughts war against us? Prayer is a great weapon. The attraction of sin pulls the mind towards evil. But when the mind takes hold of the ax of prayer and lifts it and begins to chop, it uproots even the hardest of thoughts. As long as one gets a good grip of the ax and wields it skillfully, it really brings about wonderful results.[133]

Some may remember the famous graduation speech by Navy Admiral William McRaven at the University of Texas: "If you want to change the world, start off by making your bed."[134] Christian, if you want to change the world, start off by praying. Pray the Jesus Prayer. Even when tired or feeling weary or unmotivated, pray! Persevere in prayer. Our heart may continue to feel cold. We may want to give up. *Pray!* It not perfection that God wants. It is the effort he desires. Every day, have the discipline to say the Jesus Prayer. Make it a non-negotiable practice. God sees and God knows. Never think otherwise.[135] Be deliberate and intensive. And never give up on this spiritual exercise! Never give into despair or discouragement, which are from the evil one. Christian, if you want to change the world, start off by praying.

This is our mystical Tradition, one of encountering the Risen Christ in a tangible way. Perfected by monks, who serve as spiritual guides

---

[132] *Counsels from the Holy Mountain*, 319.
[133] Ibid., 320.
[134] Admiral William McRaven, "Address to the University of Texas at Austin, Class of 2014" (YouTube).
[135] See *The Priestmonk Eusebius Giannakakis*, 274. "The personal struggle of each of you is well-known to the Lord."

through their writings and teachings, all people are encouraged to practice the Jesus Prayer. Elder Justin Pârvu of Romania said:

> Now more than ever, lay people have to pray from the heart, because this will be our only salvation. In the heart is the root of all passions and that is where we need to direct our struggles. If in the later years Christianity becomes lukewarm and superficial, we have to end all that now, this is not going to be enough anymore. If we will not pray from the heart, we will not be able to sustain the psychological attacks, because the evil one has hidden brainwashing methods that are unknown to us.[136]

Elder Eusebius would add, "Keep your mind constantly focused upon heaven and live a heavenly life. We must be thinking of God and keeping our mind with God."[137] Lord Jesus Christ, Son of God, have mercy on me, a sinner.

Practicing the Jesus Prayer

Our Gospel reading for this conference provides us with Jesus's instructions about the need to pray and persevere. We can write volumes on the necessity to pray, and its life-giving and soul-profiting benefits. However, as St. Isaac the Syrian tells us, "We cannot taste honey by reading a book."[138] God is not meant to be intellectualized; he is meant to be experienced. We could continue to discuss the history and merits of the Jesus Prayer; however, it is more important for us to experience the prayer, to taste its sweetness, and be sustained by its fruits. Let us take time to pause, to be still, and to enter into the Jesus Prayer.

---

136 Elder Justin Pârvu of Romania, posted by *Basilica News Agency*, September 14, 2022.
137 *The Priestmonk Eusebius Giannakakis*, 365.
138 See *The Ascetical Homilies of Saint Isaac the Syrian*, 153. Homily Four. "Therefore, O man, pay attention to what you read here. Indeed, can these things be known from [writings of] ink? Or can the taste of honey pass over the palate by reading books? For if you do not strive, you will not find, and if you do not knock at the door with vehemence and keep constant vigil before it, you will not be heard."

Persevere in Prayer

"The most important thing is to turn to the Prayer so that we will be united with God."[139] It is an essential element to the spiritual journey. Jesus told us this, he modeled it, and the Holy Fathers have consistently encouraged us to follow this path. If we desire to go to heaven, we need the depth of relationship with Christ that is formed through prayer, which allows us to conform our wills to the divine will. "A furnace tests gold. Prayer tests the zeal of a [person] and his love for God."[140] Elder Eusebius said:

> Mental prayer engages the heart and mind. Is it then ever possible not to lower God down to us with such power? And is it ever possible not to resolve even the most difficult problems? Even the greatest temptation can be successfully confronted in this way ... because the Lord grants the power and the grace.[141]

Once we have gained the prayer, we need to hold on to it. Elder Ephraim advised, "The struggle is not small; it does not last only one day, but until our last breath. Therefore, let us arm ourselves with the sweetest name of Jesus, so that the devil finds no room in our heart."[142] A heart emptied of the devil, his garbage, and desires for worldly things, becomes filled with Christ, becomes meek and humble,[143] and, as Romanian Father-Confessor Fr. Ciprian Grădinaru said, "Christ dwells in the heart of a humble man."[144] So let us struggle; let us labor in prayer until God sends his grace—grace that will strengthen us and guide us to heaven.[145]

---

139 St. Paisios the Athonite, "On Prayer," 173.
140 St. John Climacus, *The Ladder of Divine Ascent*, 195. Step 10: On Sleep, Prayer, and the Singing in Church of Psalms.
141 *The Priestmonk Eusebius Giannakakis*, 251.
142 *Counsels from the Holy Mountain*, 275.
143 Cf. Matt. 11:29. "Learn from me, for I am meek and humble of heart."
144 Spiritual counsel given to the author on Thursday, May 19, 2022, during a meeting at St. John Chrysostom Chapel at the entrance to the People's Salvation Cathedral, Bucharest, Romania.
145 Cf. Ibid., 334.

Lord Jesus Christ, Son of God, have mercy on me, a sinner.

Reflection

St. Seraphim of Sarov was a spiritual great-grandchild of St. Paisius Velichkovsky and is renowned as one of the greatest *staretz* in Russia. A priestmonk, he spent more than 25 years living as a hermit in a cabin near the Sarov monastery. During this time, he was attacked by robbers, who beat and left him for dead. The attack, which he did not resist, left him hunched over for the rest of his life. However, at the trial of his assailants, he pleaded to the judge for mercy on their behalf. St. Seraphim spent five months in the monastery recovering from his injuries. He then returned to the wilderness, spending 1,000 successive nights on a rock in continuous prayer with his arms raised to the sky. After living a solitary lifestyle for many years, through the inspiration of the Virgin Mary, to whom he was deeply devoted, St. Seraphim began admitting pilgrims to his hermitage as a father-confessor. He was immensely popular because of his knowledge of the interior life, healing powers, and the gift of prophecy. Hundreds of pilgrims visited him each day, also drawn by his ability to answer his guests' questions before they could ask them.

St. Seraphim was known to greet his guests saying, "Christ is risen! O my joy!" making the sign of the cross and bowing as if venerating an icon. Known, too, for his humble disposition ("Acquire a peaceful spirit and thousands around you will be saved."), he taught that the goal of the interior life was to acquire the Holy Spirit. In terms of prayer, he said:

> Among the works done for the love of Christ, prayer is the one that most readily obtains the grace of the Holy Spirit, because it is always at hand. It may happen that you want to go to church but there isn't one nearby;

or else you want to help a poor man, but you haven't anything to give, or you don't come across one; or yet again you may want to remain chaste but natural weakness prevents you from resisting temptation. But prayer is within reach of all men, and they can all give themselves to it, rich and poor, learned and unlearned, strong and weak, the sick and the healthy, the sinner and the righteous. Its power is immense; prayer more than anything else, brings us the grace of the Holy Spirit.[146]

St. Seraphim died in prayer, kneeling before an icon of the *Theotokos*. Where does prayer rank among my daily priorities? Do I make it a centerpiece of my day? Do I take time to cultivate a deeper, more personal relationship with Christ?

Reflection Questions

1. How is my relationship with Jesus? Is it a solid person-to-person relationship? Or, is it superficial? What can I do about this?

2. Prior to this retreat, what have been my experiences with the Jesus Prayer? Provide details.

3. Is the Jesus Prayer something that I should add to my personal Rule of Prayer? If not the Jesus Prayer, how do I propose to establish a deeper, more profound relationship with Christ?

---

[146] Valentine Zander, *St. Seraphim of Sarov*, trans. Sr. Gabriel Anne SSC (Crestwood, NY: St. Vladimir's Seminary Press, 1975), 86.

CONCLUSION
Recession-Proofing Our Lives

> *"I have set before you life and death, the blessing and the curse. Choose life, then, that you may live."*
> *(Deut. 30:19)*
>
> *"Your goal is holiness—the mouth, the eyes, the ears, the hands, everything—must seek holiness!"* [147]
> *(Elder Eusebius Giannakakis)*

As Christians, our hope is knowing that everything in this life will pass away, and our destiny is in the life to come. In the prevailing darkness and uncertainty of the spiritual recession that is gripping our society, we need to focus on our most important priority—investing in what matters to God and not being caught up in the noise and din of secular society, regardless of how appealing it may seem. Before us we have light and darkness, hope and despair, the blessing and the curse. Let us choose life and rejoice in hope, knowing that "God will never abandon pained souls seeking salvation."[148]

As True Christians—not ChINOs—we have been entrusted with Christ's mission, to live lives of witness, protecting ourselves from the spiritual recession. As we conclude our retreat, let us consider two final questions.

First, what can I do to keep the light of Christ burning brightly within me? I have been entrusted with this light until our Savior comes again. How can I strengthen myself for the struggles that lie ahead? What will I do to grow in holiness, preparing myself daily for the life to come? How will I deny myself, take up my cross daily, and follow Jesus?

---

147 *The Priestmonk Eusebius Giannakakis*, 406.
148 *Counsels from the Holy Mountain*, 277.

Rejoice in Hope

If heaven is our true priority, we must demonstrate our resolve to God, showing him that we truly desire the life he offers. Elder Ephraim of Arizona tell us:

> It is clear that whoever wants to walk the road of God—the road of purification, sanctification, and dispassion—must first consider the commitment he will shoulder. That is, he must be prepared to encounter temptations regardless of their origin, and to be powerfully forged in the virtue of humility.[149]

Second, what can we do as a community to be the light of Christ to a world that seems to have lost its way? "The world is far from the truth."[150] It is covered by a thick darkness, just as when clouds obstruct rays of sunlight. How do we help others find their way through the spiritual recession? People are not persuaded by words. They are drawn by authentic witness, drawn to the truth that stands in stark contrast to the falsehood of the secular world. What can we do to build up our community to keep the light of Christ burning brightly, to be a beacon of hope to the despairing, and guidance to those who desire to find the narrow gate that leads to eternal life? We are called to accompany one another on the journey.

St. Paul said, "Rejoice in hope, endure in affliction, persevere in prayer." May we be part of communities that do exactly this, strengthening others by our witness.

---

[149] Ibid., 257.
[150] Ibid., 153.

SUPPLEMENTAL INFORMATION

Calling on the Sweet Name of Jesus

The Jesus Prayer is a simple, yet powerful tool for assisting us in achieving interior stillness, overcoming temptation, and coming to know the Lord Jesus in a personal way. This is an overview of the most common form of the prayer as taught to us by our spiritual fathers.

Breathing	Prayer	Observation
Inhale	*Lord, Jesus Christ*[151]	**A profession of faith:** Acknowledging Jesus as Lord, the center of our lives and as the Son of God.
Exhale	*Son of God*	
Inhale	*Have mercy on me*	**A desire for repentance and reconciliation:** Acknowledging who we are ("a sinner") and our request of Jesus ("mercy"). In addition, the prayer is grounded in humility—the foundation for attaining all the other virtues. Humility is part of the movement away from self, surrendering self-will to the divine will.
Exhale	*A sinner*	

There are variations to this prayer. For example, some spiritual fathers advise their disciples that the prayer is said on a single breath: (Inhale) "Lord Jesus Christ, Son of God," (exhale) "have mercy on me,

---

[151] Acts 4:12: "There is no salvation through anyone else, nor is there any other name under heaven given to the human race by which we are to be saved."

a sinner." Either is acceptable, as long as the prayer itself becomes as natural as breathing. To some, the two-breath approach more readily adapts to a natural breathing pattern.

Some Greek Fathers use a shorter version: "Lord Jesus Christ, have mercy on me." Elder Ephraim of Arizona recommends that the person say this shorter Jesus Prayer at least once on inhalation and, again, in full on exhalation. Other spiritual writers exclude the phrase "a sinner," which was added later in the Russian and Slavic traditions. Each of these variants still contains the two essential components of the prayer: the invocation of the name of Jesus and the request for what we most need: mercy.

The power of this prayer is that it acknowledges a complete surrender to God, allowing Jesus to lead us on the spiritual journey to the Father. The Jesus Prayer is the only contemplative prayer tradition that approaches God with such a profound sense of humility. We need not ask for anything more than mercy because Jesus tells us, "Your Father knows what you need before you ask him."[152]

The Jesus Prayer is performed without mental forms or focusing on images, such as an icon. It does not involve imagination or any form of thoughts. Rather, it is solely intended as a means to be still and experience the presence of God. The breathing is meant to be natural, such that the prayer takes root in the heart, even when the practitioner is not conscious of it ("praying without ceasing"[153]).

For more information, see *The Fruit of Silence: The Jesus Prayer as a Foundation to the Art of Spiritual Life*, which describes the prayer and its history in more detail. Its sequel, *The Fruit of Prayer: Counsels of the Holy Fathers*, chronicles a number of spiritual practices required to cultivate the prayer.

---

[152] Matt. 6:8.
[153] Cf. 1 Thess. 5:17.

Bibliography

Ascetical Homilies of Saint Isaac the Syrian, The. Revised 2nd edition. Boston, MA: Holy Transfiguration Monastery, 2011.

Balan, Ioanichie. *Elder Cleopa of Sihastria in the Tradition of St. Paisius Velichkovsky.* Translated by Mother Cassina. Lake George, CO: New Varatec Publishing, 2001.

Bolshakoff, Sergius and M. Basil Pennington, OCSO. *In Search of True Wisdom: Visits to Eastern Spiritual Fathers.* New York, NY: Alba House, 1979.

Brianchaninov, St. Ignatius. *The Field: Cultivating Salvation.* Translated by Nicholas Kotar. Jordanville, NY: Holy Trinity Monastery Publications, 2016.

Bunderson, Carl. "Gomez Highlights Dorothy Day, Universal Call to Holiness in Final USCCB Speech." *The Pillar.* Online Edition. November 15, 2022.

Bunge, Gabriel, OSB. *Earthen Vessels: The Practice of Personal Prayer According to the Patristic Tradition.* San Francisco, CA: Ignatius Press, 2002.

Chrysostom, St. John. *On the Priesthood.* Translated by Graham Neville. Crestwood, NY: St. Vladimir's Seminary Press, 1964.

Ciobotea, Patriarch Daniel. *Confessing the Truth in Love: Orthodox Perspectives of Life, Mission, and Unity.* 2nd edition. Bucharest RO: Basilica, 2008.

———. "The One Church and the Many Churches." In *Patriarch Daniel: Rebuilding Orthodoxy in Romania.* Edited by Chad Hatfield. 36-58. Yonkers, NY: St. Vladimir's Seminary Press, 2021.

———. "The Unity between Theology and Spirituality." In *Patriarch Daniel: Rebuilding Orthodoxy in Romania.* Edited by Chad Hatfield. 13-22. Yonkers, NY: St. Vladimir's Seminary Press, 2021.

Clement of Rome, St. "Letter to the Corinthians," *The Liturgy of the Hours*, vol. 4. 448-9. New York, NY: Catholic Book Publishing Corp, 1975.

Climacus, St. John. *The Ladder of Divine Ascent*. Translated by Colm Luibheid and Norman Russell. New York, NY: Paulist Press, 1982.

Counsels from the Holy Mountain: Selected from the Letter and Homilies of Geronda Ephraim of Arizona. 2nd edition. Translated from Greek. Florence, AZ: St. Anthony's Greek Orthodox Monastery, 2020.

Cunningham, Michael. "Living the Worthy Life: Now More Than Ever We Need Jesus Christ." *Catholic365* (February 5, 2021).

Davies, Hieromonk Maximos. "Lenten Mission 2018: Hope." Delivered at St. Sophia Ukrainian Greek Catholic Church, The Colony, Texas, February 23-25, 2018.

Day, Dorothy. *The Long Loneliness: The Autobiography of Dorothy Day*. San Francisco, CA: Harper, 1952.

Didache Bible: With Commentaries Based on the Catechism of the Catholic Church. 1 edition. San Francisco, CA: Ignatius Press, 2015.

Dinan, Stephen. "Losing Our Religion: America Becoming 'Pagan' as Christianity Cedes to Culture." *Washington Times*, online, December 30, 2019.

Garrigou-LaGrange, Fr. Reginald, O.P. "Understanding Our Lord's Relentless Love," *Magnificat* 24, no. 9 (November 2022): 53-5.

Grădinaru, Fr. Ciprian. "Afterword," to Monk Moise, *The Saint of the Prisons: Notes on the Life of Valeriu Gafencu*. Translated by Monk Sava, Oașa Monastery. 278-94. Triada, 2019.

Iftimiu, Aurelian. "Patriarch Daniel Offers Remedy for Secularization during Bucharest Monastic Synaxis." *Basilica News Agency*. Online Edition. November 28, 2022.

———. "Patriarch Daniel Proclaims 2022 Solemn Year of Prayer, Commemorative Year of Hesychast Saints." *Basilica News Agency*. Online Edition. January 1, 2022.

Bibliography

Isaac of Nineveh, St. *On Ascetical Life*. Translated by Mary Hansbury. Crestwood, NY: St. Vladimir's Seminary Press, 1989.

Lewis, C. S. *Mere Christianity*. New York, NY: Harper-Collins, 1952.

_____. *The Screwtape Letters*. New York, NY: Harper Collins Publishing, 2000.

McRaven, Admiral William McRaven. "Address to the University of Texas at Austin, Class of 2014." (YouTube).

Moise, Monk. *The Saint of the Prisons: Notes on the Life of Valeriu Gafencu*. Translated by Monk Sava, Oaşa Monastery. Triada, 2019.

Nikodimos the Hagiorite, St. *Concerning Frequent Communion of the Immaculate Mysteries of Christ*. Translated by George Dokos. Thessaloniki, Greece: Uncut Mountain Press, 2006.

Paisios the Athonite, St. "On Prayer," *Spiritual Counsels*, vol. 6. Translated by Fr. Peter Chamberas. Edited by Anna Famellos and Eleftheria Kaimakliotis. Vasilika, Thessaloniki, Greece: Holy Hesychasterion Evangelist John the Theologian, 2022.

_____. "Spiritual Struggles," *Spiritual Counsels*, vol. 3. Translated by Peter Chamberas. Edited by Anna Famellos and Andronikos Masters. Souroti, Thessaloniki, Greece: Holy Monastery of Evangelist John the Theologian, 2014.

Priestmonk Eusebius Giannakakis, The. Translated by Fr. Peter A. Chambera. Montréal, QC: Alexander Press, 2021.

Pronechen, Joseph. "Archbishop Sheen's Warning of a Crisis in Christendom." *National Catholic Register*. Online Edition. July 29, 2018.

Rahner, Karl. *Foundations of Christian Faith: An Introduction to the Idea of Christianity*. Translated by William V. Dych. New York, NY: Crossroad Publishing Company, 1990.

Raya, Archbishop Joseph M. *The Face of God: Essays on Byzantine Spirituality*. Woodland Park, NJ: God With Us Publications, 2012.

_____. "Faith and Prayer," *Magnificat* 24, no. 9 (November 2022): 162-4.

Russell, Heidi. *The Source of All Love*. Maryknoll, NY: Orbis Books, 2016.

"St. Paisios the Athonite on Spiritual Warfare," *The Ascetic Experience* online (Sept. 28, 2019).

Sarah, Robert Cardinal, in conversation with Nicolas Diat. *The Day is Now Far Spent*. Translated by Michael J. Miller. San Francisco, CA: Ignatius Press, 2019.

———. *God or Nothing*. Translated by Michael J. Miller. San Francisco, CA: Ignatius Press, 2015.

———. *The Power of Silence: Against the Dictatorship of Noise*. Translated by Michael J. Miller. San Francisco, CA: Ignatius Press, 2017.

Second Vatican Council. *Dogmatic Constitution on the Church: Lumen Gentium, solemnly promulgated by His Holiness, Pope Paul VI on November 21, 1964*. In *Vatican Council II: The Basic Sixteen Documents*. General Editor, Austin Flannery, OP. 1-95. Northport, NY: Costello Publishing Company, 1996.

Sederholm, Fr. Clement. *Elder Leonid of Optina*. "The Optina Elders Series," vol. 1. Translated from Russian. Platina, CA: St. Herman of Alaska Brotherhood, 2002.

Sheldrake, Philip, *Spirituality: A Brief History*, 2nd ed. West Sussex, UK: Wiley-Blackwell, 2013.

Theophan the Recluse, St. *The Path to Salvation: A Concise Outline of Christian Ascesis*. Translated by Seraphim Rose. Stafford, AZ: The Holy Monastery of St. Paisius.

Unseen Warfare: Being the *Spiritual Combat* and *Path to Paradise* of Lorenzo Scupoli. Edited by Nicodemus of the Holy Mountain. Revised by Theophan the Recluse. Translated by E. Kadloubovsky and G. E. H. Palmer. London: Faber and Faber, 1963.

Zander, Valentine. *St. Seraphim of Sarov*. Translated by Sister Gabriel Anne, SSC. Crestwood, NY: St. Vladimir's Seminary Press, 1975.

CPSIA information can be obtained
at www.ICGtesting.com
Printed in the USA
JSHW011155090123
35932JS00003B/124